Tomatoes

By Inez Snyder

Children's Press®
A Division of Scholastic Inc.
New York / Toronto / London / Auckland / Sydney
Mexico City / New Delhi / Hong Kong
Danbury, Connecticut

Photo Credits: Cover © Shoot Pty. Ltd./Index Stock Imagery, Inc.; p. 5 © Photodisc; p. 7 © Richard T. Nowitz/Corbis; p. 9 © Kevin Fleming/Corbis; pp. 11, 15 © Ed Young/Corbis; p. 13 © Nathan Benn/Corbis; p. 17 © James L. Amos/Corbis; p. 19 © ImageState; p. 21 © Image Port/Index Stock Imagery, Inc.

Contributing Editors: Shira Laskin and Jennifer Silate
Book Design: Erica Clendening

Library of Congress Cataloging-in-Publication Data

Snyder, Inez.
   Tomatoes / by Inez Snyder.
   p. cm.—(Harvesttime)
   Includes index.
   Summary: Introduces the tomato, from the time it begins to grow on a vine until it is made into different kinds of foods.
   ISBN 0-516-27594-1 (lib. bdg.)—ISBN 0-516-25914-8 (pbk.)
   1. Tomatoes—Juvenile literature. 2. Tomatoes—Harvesting—Juvenile literature. [1. Tomatoes. 2. Harvesting.] I. Title. II. Series.

SB349.S65 2004
635'.642—dc22

2003011998

Contents

Tomatoes grow from **seeds**.

4

5

Tomato seeds are planted in large fields.

Tomatoes grow on **vines**.

The tomatoes turn red
when they are ready to
be **harvested**.

Farmers pick the tomatoes when it is warm outside.

A big **machine** helps the farmers put the tomatoes into a truck.

The truck will take the tomatoes from the field to a **warehouse**.

In the warehouse, people
pack the tomatoes
into boxes.

Then, the boxes of tomatoes
are sent to stores.

People buy tomatoes at the store.

18

19

Tomatoes are used to make many different foods.

New Words

harvested (**hahr**-vuhst-uhd) picked

machine (muh-**sheen**) something that
is made to do work or to help make
other things

seeds (**seedz**) the parts of plants that
can grow in soil and make new plants

vines (**vinez**) plants with long stems that
grow along the ground or climb trees

warehouse (**wair**-hous) a large building
used for storing goods

To Find Out More

Books
Tomatoes
by Elaine Landau
Grolier Publishing Co., Inc.

Tomatoes to Ketchup
by Inez Snyder
Scholastic Library Publishing

Web Site
Tito's Kids Corner
http://www.tomato.org/kids/index.html
Print out pictures to color and games to play about tomatoes
on this Web site.

Index

About the Author

Inez Snyder has written several books to help children learn to read. She also enjoys cooking for her family.

Reading Consultants

Kris Flynn, Coordinator, Small School District Literacy, The San Diego County Office of Education

Shelly Forys, Certified Reading Recovery Specialist, W.J. Zahnow Elementary School, Waterloo, IL

Paulette Mansell, Certified Reading Recovery Specialist, and Early Literacy Consultant, TX